FROM BABY BRAIN TO WRITER BRAIN

WRITER CHAPS – SEASON ONE

SHORT BOOKS FULL OF OUTSTANDING ADVICE FROM AUSTRALIA'S TOP SPECULATIVE FICTION WRITERS

You Are Not Your Writing and Other Sage Advice, Angela Slatter

From Baby Brain To Writer Brain: Writing Through A World of Parenting Distractions, Tansy Rayner Roberts

Eyes on the Stars: Writing Science Fiction & Fantasy, Sean Williams

The Martial Art of Writing and Other Essays, Alan Baxter

Trapping Ghosts on the Page, Kaaron Warren

FROM BABY BRAIN TO WRITER BRAIN

Writing Through A World of Parenting Distractions

TANSY RAYNER ROBERTS

Brain Jar Press
PO Box 6687
Upper Mt Gravatt, QLD, 4122
Australia
www.BrainJarPress.com

Copyright © 2021 Tansy Rayner Roberts

The moral right of Tansy Rayner Roberts to be identified as the author of this work has been asserted.

All rights reserved. No part of this book may be reproduced in any form or by any electronic or mechanical means, including information storage and retrieval systems, without written permission from the author, except for the use of brief quotations in a book review.

Cover design by Peter Ball
Cover Image: Young Mother Freelancer, Sweet Ponka/Shutterstock

ISBN: 978-0-6481761-9-0

Contents

INTRODUCTION	vii
Time To Write	1
In It For The Money	8
Balancing Act	12
Guilt	15
Not Writing	24
How On Earth Do You Get Any Writing Done?	27
Afterword	29
APPENDIX: From Baby Brain To Writer Brain in Eight Easy (hahahahaha) Weeks!	31
About the Author	47
Also by Tansy Rayner Roberts	49
Thank You For Buying This Brain Jar Press Chapbook	51

INTRODUCTION

MY BABY PUNCHED MY LAPTOP AND OTHER BEDTIME STORIES

So, how did I figure out the balance of motherhood and writing, after my first baby was born? I took it one day at a time. I eased myself into it. I let myself breathe. Once I returned to the keyboard, I trusted myself to know my limits. I wrote a little bit more every day. I built momentum. I built productivity…

And then one day, as I was sitting on the couch and typing busily away, my baby punched my laptop. Not a gentle smack, or a tap. It was a flat-out punch.

(The laptop and the baby were both fine.)

Still, it was a shock to my system. All my parenting guilt and non-productivity guilt combined into one huge mass of feelings. Was I trying to do too much?[1] Had I traumatised or neglected my child?[2] Should I stop writing altogether?

That was the big question, really. My identity was so closely wrapped up in being a writer, that I couldn't imagine not doing it. Everything changes when you have kids, sacrifices are a constant fact of reality … but did I have to sacrifice this, too?

I didn't quit writing. I didn't give up the idea that

someday writing would be my real, 'proper' job, though at the time I had only a couple of published novels from years earlier, a short list of published short stories, and a long list of rejections.

I was used to the idea that parenting a small child was going to affect my writing time and productivity, but the day my baby punched my laptop was the first time I seriously considered whether my commitment to writing was going to affect how good a parent I was. It was a confronting, terrifying idea.

Holding yourself to an impossible standard of perfection is just as damaging with creative work as it is with parenting. But from that point forward, my personal criteria for competent parenting was 'don't let your kid develop a sibling rivalry with your work tools.'[3]

Years later, around about the time that my Eldest started school, I had a second baby. This was one of the most active points of my writing career. I was in the middle of producing a trilogy of fantasy novels for a major publishing house ... and I had a new baby.

This time around I couldn't slowly ease into a writing routine after a lengthy maternity break: I had to hit the ground running. I wrote. I edited. I blogged *all the time*.[4] Sometimes I updated my old LiveJournal three times a day!

While hitting my deadlines, keeping two children alive and occasionally finding moment to breathe in and out, I also chronicled a really important time in my life: the era of writing lots while my children were small. Thanks to the intensity and lack of filter in the blogging process, I was surprisingly honest about my guilt, worries and failings. I don't know that I'd be so open now, if I was writing about these topics from scratch ... and let's face it, without the blog to look back on, I wouldn't remember most of it!

INTRODUCTION

This book consists of carefully chosen (and rewritten) essays about parenting (while they're little) and writing, and how I managed to get through all that to where I am now: with chill older children, a day job, more books under my belt and still, somehow, a messy house.

How did I do it? Imperfectly.

I failed a lot. I struggled a lot. And you know? Looking back on it, maybe I should have just napped more.

But my proudest achievements in my life are my kids, and my books. Talking about them has always been my favourite thing to do. So here we go.

---

1. Well, yes, obviously.
2. I have it on good authority from my now-teenager that actually, less parental attention would have been appreciated.
3. Ironically, my second baby developed violent tendencies towards every paper book I attempted to read during the first year of her life. I should just count my blessings that both kids took out their frustrations on inanimate objects instead of each other...
4. Can you believe there was a whole decade where we just blogged constantly?

Time To Write

I have a confession to make.

I let my writing muscles atrophy.

It took me a while to realise and accept that this was what had happened. At the time, thanks to a major multi-novel contract with a Big Name Publisher, I had been leaping from deadline to deadline. There's something sparkly and marvellous about a deadline imposed upon you from someone else — not only do they pay you, but there's also a level of accountability in it that I find personally inspiring.

Having a baby in the middle of process meant that the deadlines grew harder and harder to reach[1], but I persevered even as the deadlines for different books started imposing on each other with editing and first draft and second draft all overlapping. I got through it.

Then the trilogy was over, and it was time to start again.

The deadlines from other people began to drift further and further apart, and at first I didn't notice. I had time to write new things! A novel I really wanted to write had netted me two separate grants. Hooray, I had time to write it! Better yet, I could take the time I needed to make it good.

I think 'time to write' must be one of the most misleading phrases in the English language. Because even though I had two paid days of daycare a week, and my older child in full time school, and financial support, even though my baby was finally sleeping through the night... somehow none of the time I should have had available was translating into 'time to write.'

('How do you do it all?' they ask. 'You must be really disciplined,' they say. 'I'd love to have time to write a book.')

Oh, I wrote. I wrote myself in slow circles, trying to find the new book. I told myself it was only hard because it was the first new project I had started for five years. I told myself that I had plenty of time.

"Plenty of time," by the way, is even worse than "time to write". Because if you have plenty of time ... why aren't you writing?

I knew from past experience that I was capable of writing fast, in great heaping piles of words that were somehow, magically, pretty good. My first drafts were clean. My word counts were high.

But that was then, and this was now.[2]

It took me a long time to come to terms with the fact that this, the first new novel I was working on after my big trilogy, was just not flowing. There was something wrong with the beginning, that had to be fixed. Then something wrong with chapter three. You can't move ahead when chapter three isn't perfect, right, right?

I used to be good at this. My expectations were based on my memories of previous achievements. But halfway through the year, I still couldn't hit that first 20K mark, let alone a second, or a third. I had bought into my own image of the kind of writer I was, and assumed somehow that That Person would get the book written. While I was getting the other stuff done.

When you only have two days of paid daycare a week[3], it's horribly easily to over-estimate how much you can get done in those days. Like, your week's worth of writing, AND catching up on the housework, AND taking your older kid to after school activities, AND picking up things from the post office, exercising, reading, sewing, planning dinner, shopping, etc.[4]

And then you remember, hang on, two days of daycare, once you deduct the time on either side of the school day for the older child ... that's actually only five and a half hours, twice a week.

And maybe you need to write more than that.

Maybe (this time in a very, very tiny voice), maybe you should be writing EVERY FREAKING DAY.

Write Every Day is one of the more controversial of Heinlein's famous writing rules.[5] Many writers are understandably scathing about the concept of writing every day because a) they are well practiced and disciplined enough not to need rules like that and b) they understand only too well that forcing yourself to write every day is a good way to fill your novels up with time-wasting nonsense, padded words that only existed because you guilted yourself into writing them.

Rules only work for you if and when they work for you.

On the other hand, Write Every Day had worked for me before.

FLASHBACK

Remember that big trilogy, the one with the deadlines? It almost didn't get written at all. I was working on the very first novel when I was pregnant with my first child. I was also trying to finish my doctorate. The pregnancy gave me one hell of a deadline to meet, and I reluctantly sacrificed my beloved half-finished novel to get the thesis done before I became a mother.

I didn't make it.

Probably one of the first times in my life that I failed to meet a really, really important deadline.

So, I went on maternity leave from my doctorate, I had my baby, I learned how to be a parent and so on. Eventually I came back and finished my thesis and then, finally, more than a year after I stopped, I returned to fiction writing and found it nearly impossible.

The difference in my life before parenthood and after was too great. I couldn't even remember how writing fiction worked, let alone hold a whole story in my head.

What saved me was a challenge I have since recommended over and over to writing students, to friends, to random strangers who tell me they are going to write a novel *when they have the time.*

The challenge is this: 100 words a day for 100 days, in an unbroken line. The words can be anything. The point is getting words on the page. It's the equivalent, I imagine, to those first practice laps you start to walk before running when training for a marathon.[6] One day at a time. Every day.

Small achievable goals. Telling yourself to write every day when you mean a chapter a day ... that's rough. But 100 words a day? It's doable. It's achievable. You can do it even if you've forgotten all day, and it's bedtime.

I don't know that I ever made it to the 100 days. I think I got as far as 49, forgot a day, started again, got to 70 something, forgot a day, and rage-quit. But by that time, I'd written a little something every day for 70+days, and that was enough to get me back into the mindset of being a working writer.[7]

I found my way back to writing, I finished my novel, I

sold my novel as a trilogy to a big publisher, and I relaunched my career. It all started with 100 words a day.

FLASH FORWARD

Here I was again, years later, on the other side of at least massive writing and publishing (and reinvention of myself) achievement, and it felt like I was back at the beginning.

Because I was.

I'm not going to say that finishing a major fantasy trilogy while editing the previous books and having a new baby and all those things at once actually broke me ... but getting to the end of that process kind of did.

However stressful those intense external deadlines had been when I was slamming through them on next to no sleep, there was also a freedom in them because for several years I had no time to waste. Once those deadlines relaxed, my brain[8] slid way too far in the other direction.

Over the first six months of writing my new, post-trilogy book, I went from being one of those super professional deadline-hitting authors into the kind of writer who wishes she had Time To Write.

So, that was embarrassing.

I decided to get my act together. I had let my writing muscles atrophy, to the point where even getting 200 words on the page was painful, and boring, and made me want to do housework. *Housework*, people! I had forgotten how to be a writer.

Luckily, I knew what I had to do.

I had to practice. I had to build my writing muscles through regular exercise. I had to pretend to be a writer hard enough that I fooled the universe and myself.

So, I signed up to an online write-a-thon, giving myself the challenge of 5000 words a week. My plan was to write

1000 words a day for five days in a row, collapse for the weekend.[9] Then do it again, and again.

Why yes, this was a much tougher exercise than that whole 100 words a day business. But I was impatient with myself, and sure that I could do it.

The first day was agony. Every 200 hundred words made my head spin. Seriously, how had my writing attention span got so low? It used to be I could easily get to 800 or even 1200 words before I started double checking my total and admiring the weather out the window.

My husband actually watched me on the second day, as he was home from work with a cold. He was horrified. It was, admittedly, gruesome. Sixty words in, I was whining for a cup of tea and coming up with excuses to skip the day altogether. 'What the hell happened to you?' he asked.

Fair comment.

The third day was better. I went to Pilates in the morning and spent a lot of the time thinking about the novel that had not only completely taken over my brain, but was now demanding I re-structure it from scratch.

I will, I told it, *but only after I've written my 1000 words for the day.* After Pilates, I came home and did exactly that.

If there's a moral to this story, it has nothing to do with Heinlein's Pompous Rules For Writers With Endless Resources. Instead, I will borrow from all those aerobics tapes I watched in the 90s: Move It, Or Lose It.

If you don't write regularly, it gets harder to write.

When people talk about time to write, either having it or not having it, the part they always miss out is that extra verb. You have to *find* time to write. You have to make time to write. Sometimes, you have to beg, borrow and steal time to write.

If time to write is not happening for you, you have to change the universe until it does. And the easiest way to do that is to find a regular habit you can realistically stick to, and stick to it.

One word in front of the other. Rinse, repeat, until done. Then do it again.

---

1. And I occasionally had to move one or two.
2. Also in the before times, I was capable of reading 200 books a year ... after my first child that dropped to around 25-50 but it took me a long time to recalibrate which is why my house is STILL, fifteen years later, full of books I'll never have time to read.
3. A luxury for many work-from-home parents.
4. And mostly failing at a lot of those things too.
5. The others being "Finish Everything You Start" and "Submit Everything You Finish".
6. Let's not pretend I know how marathons work other than their primary function in our society: as a useful simile for something very, very hard.
7. It's somewhere around this point that my baby punched my laptop.
8. Which clearly needed a holiday.
9. To this day, collapsing on the weekend remains a goal I am rarely able to earn.

In It For The Money

Something I think about a lot is how money is a currency, and time is a currency, and the two currencies don't always have a straightforward exchange rate.

Here's the thing: I'm a working writer, and the day I became a stay-at-home mother was the day it finally occurred to me that I didn't have to be a full-time writer. Letting go of the idea of ever earning a full-time income from my writing was hugely freeing for me, because earning a *part-time* income felt much more achievable and realistic.

Even now, fifteen years later, I'm not a full-time writer[1], though every time I stop and count up all the jobs I actually have, it's hard to believe I am one person.

The thing that infuriates me most about conversations around writing/art and money is how many people believe that expecting to be paid a reasonable and sustainable amount of money in exchange for art is somehow unfair, like treating your art as a business is selling out.[2]

Money matters. Paying artists matters. Too often, writers and artists are sent out into the world without any kind of business background, because there's this stupid romantic idea that as soon as you start treating your art like a business, it stops being art.

Personally, I'm in it for the money. Oh, don't get me wrong. I don't crave mansions or film deals or any of that largesse. But if I can't earn an income from my writing, then how can I justify spending so much time doing it?

I've been incredibly lucky to have a partner who supported me financially during my university years, and when our children were smaller. I also had a small business I ran with my mother, which continues to this day. I taught night classes in creative writing. I worked casual hours in big bursts a few of times a year, supervising exams, to supplement all the other bits and pieces of my scattered income.

These days, have a part-time job I love, as well as a moderate but comfortable part-time writing income, and the balance is working very well for me.

When my kids were small, the currency I thought about most was not money, but time. Our budget allowed us to put our youngest in daycare two days a week until school age, which gave me time to work. But the hours I spent writing weren't just taken from the daycare jar, they were pinched and borrowed from our daily life. The time I spent writing was time I didn't spend with my children, or cleaning the kitchen, or organising the cupboards, or working on my other small business, or applying for part-time work that would pay me at a much better rate!

I don't believe that the perfect mother is one who spends 24 hours a day with her children[3], but when my kids were tiny I was constantly aware that the time I spent writing was taken away from them.

I couldn't justify that to myself if it was just about the art. 'I'm making art here, sweetie, so no, you can't finger-paint, because it would take too much time to clean up, and it's either I cook dinner OR I clean the floors, not both, because I'm busy over here. Making art.'

People[4] who work outside the home for an employer can justify it more easily because it's a traditional concept of work, and most people understand it. You get paid for doing a thing. The money pays for your family to eat. It's basic and essential.[5]

I could barely justify time to myself to read a book or drink a cup of tea, in the days before my kids were both in full time school. Looking back, it feels like a brief window in my life, but at the time it was a yawning, endless chasm. The only way I could justify pouring time into my stories was by thinking of it as a business, as an investment in our future. As something that could potentially earn me at least the equivalent of minimum wage.

In a perfect world, art for art's sake would be a currency all on its own. But we're not living in that world right now.

I've won awards, which helps me feel like I'm not wasting my time. I've had lovely reviews, and warm conversations with readers. I've been to festivals and conventions that make me feel like a real writer. I've had wonderful experiences that have inspired me to write more, better stories.

But there's nothing quite as inspiring to me as writing a thing and getting paid for it. As another human being deciding that it's worth paying for a thing you wrote, whether it's a $10,000 book advance, a $250 cheque for a story, a $5 pledge to Patreon, or a 99¢ ebook sale.

Money matters to artists. It's not everything, but it matters, and anyone who tells you otherwise is selling something.

---

1. Or a full-time anything.

2. This raised its particularly ugly head all over again during the Covid-19 shutdowns in 2020, with the clear message that millions of people expect to be entertained for free in a time of crisis, but look askance at creative people who want to be compensated for their time, effort, skill and work.
3. I know I would be far less than perfect as a parent if I tried doing that!
4. Let's face it, fathers.
5. I'm not saying that working mothers don't feel guilt or cop criticism for working outside the house when their kids are small, but that's another book …

Balancing Act

Let's talk about weekends.

I've spent most of my working life as a freelancer, and the only way for a freelancer to take a weekend is to physically pick it up and run away with it, laughing maniacally like a bandit.

Whenever I see newbies starting down the freelance road, whether they're stay at home parents who plan to keep writing, or Real Job people who are transitioning to work-from-home or post-doctoral work, well ...

My advice is always, take your weekends.

It's not as easy as it sounds. My own relationship with weekends has been fraught and complicated my whole life, and it only became more so when I had kids.

No one gives you structured days off, when you are your job. You have to give them to yourself.

These days, I have two main jobs aside from parenting: my freelance writing/self-publishing business funded by book sales and crowdfunding, and a part-time job with a real boss and paid hours.[1]

One of these jobs — guess which one — stops on

weekends. The other one is endless and forever, tucked around the edges of everything else that I do.

Every now and then, when life gets to be over-complicated and stressful, I have to take a deep breath, recalibrate my systems, and restore my weekends as actual time off instead of an active part of my working week. Even if that means taking time away from my business, my creative work, and so on.

When my kids were little, weekends were the only times that I had a co-parent home all day, sharing the load. I had another adult around to deal with kid-issues and that took a lot of strain off me. The downside was, as always, my own expectations.

I would regularly fall into the bad habit of assuming the weekend would be more productive work-wise than was realistic. Then I'd start out on Monday feeling way behind, over-worked, under-achieved.

A day in which you get nothing done is not the same as a scheduled day off. One is a frustrating ball of aargh, and the other is a potentially restful necessity.

These days, my life has changed a lot. My husband has retired, and is home all day. My kids are off at school and after school activities — but I have a co-parent around full time to help with driving and commitments and chores and emergencies. I have less pressure around the immediate necessities of parenting-while-working.

But also, I have a day job.

Weekends now are the time when every family member is home, often doing their own thing ... and with me released from the day job commitments, those two precious days start looking like the best possible time to catch up on all my writing and publishing work.

Unfortunately, my kids are also now old enough to call me out for working on weekends, when they remember I exist. There's housework to be done, and baths to be sorted out. Visitors are scheduled. Parties are planned. Soccer games must be planned for. Lazy pyjamas are required.

The details of life change from year to year, but the balancing act for the creative worker who is also a parent is a constant challenge. Flexibility is important. *Weekends are important*.

When I plan out my month and everything I want to achieve in it, I try to at least *start out* not scheduling work for weekends. They're my break-out space and, more often than not, that's where a lot of my work does get done. All those things I thought I'd have time to do during the week, and did not.

It's an incredibly imperfect system.

But even if I finish every month having worked a lot on the weekends ... it's still important to me that I don't have high expectations that those will ever be productive days.[2] If my 5-day schedule blows out to a 6- or 7-day schedule, that's at least manageable. If I start by packing expectations into all 7 days, there's nowhere to go ... unless there are pocket dimensions with extra days packed away in them?

Let me know if you find one.

---

1. Swoony sigh: I get paid the same amount for every hour I work within a fortnight of doing that work, it's like *magic*.
2. This also applies to school holidays, and those odd days between Christmas and New Year, which somehow I always believe will contain a portal of endless productivity ...

Guilt

I started taking weekly Pilates classes when I was 31, six months after my second child was born. I did it because all of a sudden, it felt like every writer I knew who was 10 years older than me and/or 10 years ahead in their careers was suddenly falling by the wayside, toppled (or at least extremely restricted) by back pain, RSI, arthritis, or some combination of the three, all caused by those long hours typing.

It seemed like most people at Pilates were there to fix something awful they had done to their bodies (or that their bodies had done to them, I guess). I felt a bit abashed about being there pre-emptively, but a decade later, can I just say that was a *good* call. Well done, me.

Pilates was something I had to circumvent a lot of guilt to allow myself to do — because it was something clearly of benefit to myself rather than the family. This was especially hard for me when I was using household money to pay for my classes — slightly less so once we had a budget rehaul, and I was able to pay for them myself.

I know, by the way, that I shouldn't have to justify it, and what's good for me is good for the family and so on, but logic is logic and guilt is guilt.

Managing guilt is a huge aspect of being a working mother. Or a mother full stop, I guess. It's also one of the hardest aspects to reconcile with being a feminist — what works in theory often falls down in practice, and when the baby's screaming, theory doesn't help! I find it interesting when talking to other mothers that we all have different lines of guilt, those which we cross regularly and feel bad about, those which we try not to cross and feel awful about, and those which have come to terms with.

I'm using the specifically gendered term "mother" here rather than "parent" not just because I'm cis-female myself, but also because for women, the relationship between parenting, work, guilt and expectations comes with a specific extra load of emotional and practical challenges. Men have their own challenges around work and parenting and public perception, particularly those men who take on a larger percentage of parenting than society deems acceptable, but I can't speak to those as comfortably.

Certainly the judgement levelled at women for their balance of work and care is especially damaging because there is no way to "win". And believe me, no matter how harsh the expectations/double standard of society ... we mothers often judge ourselves even harder.

One of my firm personal lines early was not to use paid daycare for Pilates. I only had two days a week, and I needed those days for writing! I also used that time for shopping, housework, chores, etc. but I was well aware of how much writing and writing-related work I had to do that didn't quite fit into those brief bursts of time.

I considered myself lucky that I never felt guilty about sending my kids to daycare, despite the opinions of those who felt that I should. I felt extra lucky that my kids loved daycare and benefited from it.[1] Our local centre was a really good one, convenient to my house.

At one point we considered dropping one of those daycare days, because it was such a huge expense. But one was not enough. I desperately needed the mental clarity that came from those precious hours of not having a small child in the house. This ramped up the level of guilt associated with those days — which meant in turn that I always felt the pressure to make them REALLY, REALLY PRODUCTIVE.

That is what we call Useful Guilt.

This is my own way of looking at the world. Other people can spend their daycare days however they like! Mother/parent guilt is incredibly personal. Like body image, it's amazing how many women can be deeply critical of themselves and yet happily encourage others to not feel bad at all, without noticing the disconnect.

So, I could not let myself use half of a paid daycare day for a Pilates class. Instead, I fell back on that great resource of the privileged working mother: unpaid labour from our parents.

My mother was hugely supportive of me taking my class and choosing something to prioritise my health and wellbeing. So she arrived on my doorstep once a week to mind the baby. It was a dream arrangement — she got to spend time with her grandchild, it could continue through the school holidays with the school-age kid too, and because my mother was flexible, I was able to extend my Pilates class into getting other chores done, parcels posted, PO Box checked, and even occasionally having lunch out. Plus she always did my washing up, and sometimes cleaned the floor too. MY MOTHER IS AWESOME.[2]

It wasn't just my mother contributing her time to help me manage mine, when the kids were small. My dad also chipped in with at least one school pick up a week, which extended one of my paid daycare days to 7.5 hours child-free. He continued that long after daycare was a distant memory.

A lot of parenting is about juggling time, and money, and never quite having enough of either. Those years of paid daycare taught me a lot about how to value my time. They added a certain pressure not only for me to be personally productive, but to expect to be paid for my work. I started thinking a lot harder before doing favours for people, or volunteering time.

One of my biggest parenting guilt stories has a happy ending. I always felt bad that I rarely volunteered parent help to the primary school. It's one of those things that is expected of us "at home" parents.[3] I kept my contributions to things that could be done outside school hours — the sorts of things that actually, working parents often choose over classroom help because they're *at work*.

Somehow the idea that I was also at work, despite working from home, kept slipping away from me.

This issue came to ahead recently when my now teenaged eldest informed my youngest child that, actually, 'Every single time Mum came to school was hugely embarrassing.'

Readers, I have never felt so relieved in my life. It was like a massive burden of guilt was lifted off my shoulders. My kids, who love me dearly[4], had given me a great gift.

If I'd been told my presence was embarrassing ten years earlier, it would have been even more helpful!

There are so many potential issues, problems, and complications tangled up in the concepts of Guilt and Motherhood, Guilt and Writing Time, Balancing Paid Work and Writing, Balancing Unpaid Work and Writing, that I think it's impossible for any person to sum it up in an all-encompassing way. I always find it interesting to read other people's stories about how they handle that difficult balance:

how they deal with their own expectations, and the expectations of others, which are often sharply gendered.

Your story is going to be different, not only depending on whether you are male, female or non-binary, but also whether you are partnered, who works outside the house, who doesn't, how much housework you do, whether or not you have kids, how old the kids are, what their needs are, and just how clean you (or your partner) feel the house has to be anyway. It changes as circumstances change.

Ten years ago, with a partner who worked outside the home and paid most of our essential bills, I agonised over what I didn't do as much as what I did do. I felt the weight of housework left undone far more sharply than he did … and in circumstances when having a messy house was inconvenient, I felt that an unreasonable share of the blame for our domestic chaos was down to me.

I did not, let us be clear, feel quite so bad about the domestic situation that I actually stopped writing to do more housework. Which is how I got so many books written.

These days, with a retired partner with far more leisure time than I have, with older children who really should pull more weight without being asked, my guilt has taken a back seat. We have visitors coming soon. I should be cleaning the house right now. I'm not. I'm editing an essay about domestic guilt. I REGRET NOTHING.

When your kids are young, you worry about all the little things you might do to screw them up, or make them resent you, or endanger their health and happiness. As they get older, particularly with younger siblings who get the "benefit" of parents who have learned which parts of parenting *not* to worry about, a lot of that stress floats away. Usually because the actual problems that come with being a parent are specific to who you and your children are as people. The abstract parental worries carry less weight …

and that makes room for all your personalised parental drama!

I became a better parent once I internalised the idea that children need to learn to value and respect the work done by their parents, and to see that their parents have lives and needs outside the immediate domestic circle. They also, incidentally, need to value domestic work done on their behalf, and ideally see this modelled by adults of all genders. I was being a good role model by running a business and making time for my writing as well as making sure they actually ate lunch during the school holidays! Look at me go!

Having something which is yours, that keeps you fulfilled in between the frantic work and drudgery and fairy dust of being a parent, undoubtedly makes you a better parent as long as there's no actual neglect of the children. It doesn't have to be writing. But if you don't have something of your own, you might disappear entirely into the job of being there for your kids. Like all forms of self-employment, art included, domesticity will absorb all the time & resources you put into it, and then some.

The parenting-of-small-children window, in which it feels like they need everything from us, is finite. Their needs change. Their independence grows. The job of caring for them while they are small is one designed to end in redundancy.

When my kids were little, I spent huge amounts of mental energy justifying time I took for myself. Earning money for my writing helped me manage my guilt about not doing enough for my kids ... and the hard grind of caring for a baby, especially the second time around, lifted a lot of guilt off my shoulders about not contributing equally to the household from a financial point of view.

Why did I need to feel guilty at all? Possibly, if I'd been

willing to spend time and money, I could have gone to therapy to figure all that out. I wrote books instead.

The idea that your time does not belong to you, that other people are entitled to more than their fair share of it, is a thoroughly dangerous one, and yet as the work-from-home parent of a family unit, it's amazing how quickly that idea can eat you alive. Many people — especially women — find themselves called to family duties to a point that any leisure or creative time feels like a selfish luxury.

We just lived through 2020, the year of corona virus, the year of lockdowns. And what did we see here in Australia?

- Artists, especially those working in performance, were the first to be affected by financial losses and industry shutdowns, but nearly the last to be considered for financial support from governments (Many never received support).
- At a time when more people than ever were bingeing media content and finally catching up on their to-read piles, artists and writers not only donated huge amounts of time and resources to fundraising and free content projects, but were also called out as selfish for expecting to be paid for their work, and for enforcing copyrights.
- Parents in lockdown were expected to do double duty of managing their kids' school commitments and education, while continuing their own work from home ... and this pressure fell disproportionately on women.
- Teachers were told repeatedly that their job was entirely about babysitting-for-the-sake-of-the-economy, while also being asked to educate children under far more challenging circumstances

than ever before, across multiple platforms and spaces, with minimal resources.
- One of the first budget (and risk-management) choices made by many households was to drop their paid household cleaner without compensation.
- Childcare was only made free during a period of time when most people were (legitimately) too cautious to use it, and was the first industry to lose government subsidy.

Basically, we learned that no one wanted to pay for art, childcare or cleaning services … and yet they wanted all those things to magically exist as an endless resource for everyone else's benefit.

We were told that writers, at least, weren't suffering like other workers, because people were still buying books in lockdown, and we were used to working from home.

But everywhere I looked, my creative worker friends were stressed, exhausted, parented-out, distracted, interrupted, and utterly unable to reach their usual levels of productivity in making and sharing art.

None of us wrote our great lockdown novel.

No one wrote King Lear.

The media blasted us about the stresses on iso-school parents, assuring us that our children wouldn't suffer if we were really, really bad at it, ignoring the reality that so many of us, and our kids, were already coping very badly indeed with an impossible situation … while others were actually doing okay (and maybe feeling guilty about that, too).

Where I live right now, lockdown has ended, the kids are

back in school (for now), and life has returned to something like normal.

I have half an hour before I have to pick up my kid from soccer practice.

I should probably spend that half hour cleaning the house.

But if I let it stay messy, I can keep working on this book.

---

1. It's frustrating to me that when discussing my kids being in daycare, I always felt the need to emphasise straight away how much that kid enjoyed it, and the direct benefit they got from going there, rather than acknowledging my own needs. Pre-emptive defensiveness is one of those fun things that goes hand-in-hand with mother guilt, of course.
2. Ahem, this is where I admit that, more than a decade later, with my kids in full time school now, and my retired husband home to keep an eye on them in the holidays if needed, my mother still visits on Pilates Day. It is a joyous family tradition.
3. A lot of things are expected of 'at home' parents, regardless of what our actual work commitment is during those hours.
4. As long as I stay in my proper place, which is apparently anywhere but school.

Not Writing

One of the most important skills to hone as a writer is the gentle art of Not Writing.

It's easy to get caught up in metrics — word count means progress, books only get written if you regularly put your bum in your seat and type, etc. etc. Those things are true. But it's also important to recognise when you're drained and need to refill the well, or when you're pushing too hard at a project that needs to simmer, not boil.

For me, this becomes obvious when the writing gets hard. Writing is not always easy for me. Writing every day is certainly not easy, with my intense time pressures. But there's a huge difference between a slow, painful stop-and-start march through a writing project, and hitting that stride: the beautiful momentum that for me rarely fires up until a consistent month or so of writing the same thing.

It's glorious when the words fly, and the story becomes fierce, and the words fall out of my fingers.

And sometimes — more and more, these days — I can't get to that point. I can hit word counts, but each word is hard-won. And that means there's something wrong. Not *wrong* wrong, but definitely not right.

When that happens, it's time to rest. To *not write* — on that particular novel, at least. To not prioritise word count. To allow myself to feel productive even if I'm not hitting a target each week.

And that's the hard part. Because I know myself, and if I don't feel productive then chances are I'm going to start feeling really bad about myself, and that makes it harder to be creative.

But hitting the word count regularly isn't the only thing a novel (or a novella, or a story) needs to get finished. Sometimes I need to stop, breathe and redefine what "productive" is going to mean, that week or that month.

Maybe I need to research all manner of things about the Victorian era, or Arthurian myth. Maybe I need to read a bunch of gothic novels, or space opera, or Roman history. Maybe I need to walk away and let the story cook in the back of my brain. As Jenny Crusie would say, I need to let the girls in the basement take over — those helpful supernatural pixies who do all the grunt work in the subconscious while you're not paying attention.

This is a trick, obviously. Because what I'm hoping is that by forcing myself to Not Write, I will instantly refuel my novel and my creative juices, returning both to peak condition.

I want the next time I write to be because I'm hurting to write, because the story is screaming its way out of my head. And I'm really hoping that allowing myself this Not Writing period means that I will sneakily end up ahead of myself, because the next bout of writing will come faster, better, stronger.

What I'm really bad at is allowing this time of Not Writing

to count in my head as work. Because that's a slippery slope towards 'ah me yes I need to watch this box set of DVDs which counts as work, and also I need a coffee, and oh whoops, I didn't write a novel this year, how did that happen?'

The danger to taking a break from writing is how easy it is to get swept up in the daily and domestic, in all the little jobs that have to be done. To lose what writing muscles I have all over again.

My solution, most of the time, is to write Something Else. But this system, too, has its flaws.

There's a difference between not writing and Not Writing. There's also a difference between lounging around in front of the TV, and Productive Thinking Time. The clever thing is figuring out what that difference is.

As with all writing methods, it's a work in progress. As am I.

How On Earth Do You Get Any Writing Done?

People ask: 'How on earth do you get any writing done?'

And I reply with varying degrees of humour and goodwill:

- 'I don't. Have you seen how many books *other* writers can get done in a year?'
- 'Panic = adrenalin.'
- 'I'm a really bad housewife.'
- 'Daycare helps.'
- 'My mum cleans my house.'
- 'Full time school is basically magic.'
- 'Oh, well, you know.'

This is the answer I never give:

- 'If I don't write, I won't write, and that's not an option for me. What do you people *who don't write* do with all that time pouring out of your ears?'

Mostly when people ask how I get my writing done, I

resist the urge to laugh bitterly in their faces, and then I compose a tactful answer, so as not to make them feel bad because they *don't* write novels in their own "spare time". I fail to take the credit for all the work I do, **not to mention the effort I put into making sure my work happens**.

When you love something, you make time for it. You stuff down the guilt, you roll up your sleeves and you get it done.

I chew pieces off the ends of other pieces of time, and jam them all together with sticky tape. I never stop and smell the roses, because I'm too busy trying to squeeze my time dry, three times over. I have no hobbies that aren't, somehow, also work. Sometimes I let my kids watch too much TV. I never do enough housework. I don't get enough exercise. I expect a lot of my partner.

I write because I write because I write.

Afterword

No one is "ready" to be a parent.

No one has "time" to write a novel.

Do your best.

Take deep breaths.

Allow yourself to have weekends.

And then, all things being well, if you have balanced your writer self and parent self with a basic level of competence …

Then, like me, you may someday be rewarded by a bright-eyed child saying to you with confidence: 'I want to be a writer when I grow up!'

And an icy chill of dread will take over your whole body.

But you just keep smiling. Because no one needs ever know that, just for a moment, you almost replied: 'You know you'll need a real job too, right?'

Unless you write about it in a book.

APPENDIX: From Baby Brain To Writer Brain in Eight Easy (hahahahaha) Weeks!

Becoming a parent for the second time is harder than the first time in exactly the same way that writing a second novel in a series is harder than the first. With your first book, you might make the most mistakes along the way, but you also have what feels (in retrospect) like an impossibly decadent amount of time to get it right: to play and experiment and enjoy the experience. To learn. To be creative.

But writing a second book while you're still editing the first, because it hasn't been released yet, and there's still so much work to be done on and around that first book, but you need literally every scrap of energy (that you don't have) to work on the second one?

Wow, it's not so much a perfect metaphor as a description of *literally what I was going through in 2009.*

On three hours sleep a night.

The following is the only slightly edited journal of my eight (cough) week program to return to the world of deadlines, edits and Actual Proper Writing after the birth of my second child, in the middle of writing the Creature Court trilogy. I think you'll find it educational. I know I did.

THE JOURNAL BEGINS

I've been wanting to document my recent attempts to return to writing after having a baby. The biggest difference between Eldest's babyhood and Youngest's is that I have to start working much sooner. Last time I had an unfinished PhD hanging over my head, and at least three months leave before I had to start thinking about using my brain again. I didn't seriously start working again for six. It was even longer before I started writing fiction again — I wrote one short story that year, and before I could pick up my abandoned novel project[1]. I had to challenge myself with '100 words a day for 100 days' to get back to writing regularly.

This time around, I have professional writing deadlines. I am contracted to produce Book #2 by 1 January. If I take three months off... well, yeah. I'm gonna run badly out of time. Also, rewrites and edits for Book #1 are going to be swooping by at some point. I suspect that my 'best case scenario' plan which included drafting Book #3 in November is looking unrealistic.

I have 90K already drafted, so I should be in good shape to finish Book #2 and "make it write good" as long as I can get my brain back and working to full capacity by the end of September. Um. Which is soon. Also, the end of September marks the end of my co-parent's leave options. So I'll be a full-time mother of two. Eeeeep.

WEEK ONE

Hahahaha no. Productivity and the writer brain was not a priority. Most of this week passed in a haze. Though I do think I should get bonus points for completing a set of edits for a novella the day before my waters broke. I did start thinking writerly thoughts again during some of the night-feeding fog, but sadly they were for the wrong book — i.e. the one I want to pitch and write after this trilogy is done. Damn it!

WEEK TWO

Sanity is possibly closing in on me. Certainly I am physically more able than I was a week ago, so I can go out in public without falling apart after an hour or so. I'm reading more, and while the nights aren't really any easier (ha, lucky to get one three-hour session a night), my brain is I think adapting. Or something. Yesterday was very exciting because Youngest lay on her quilt under the new (hand-me-down) baby gym and occupied HERSELF while awake for about twenty minutes without being held or attached to one of her parents. Ahh, the future, it is a happy place.

Writing-wise, my brain has been buzzing with ideas, framing scenes and sending me hunting for research books. Um. For the WRONG FREAKING NOVEL. Yep, that future-beyond novel is rearing its head again, demanding attention.[2] I have had a few other hints that my writing brain might be trickling back. I've managed to put a few book reviews together, I've finished up the roleplaying threads I was in the middle of writing when the baby arrived, and I'm finally writing this blog entry.

I have one more week of August left and then I really seriously want to be dipping my toe back into the Big Trilogy. Even if I don't really want any of those characters anywhere near my baby. Back, fiends! Oh, and while I'm yelling at fictional characters, Stay away, Mercutio and Rosaline, I will get to you in a year or so.[3]

Stay tuned.

WEEK THREE

Two big breakthroughs this week - I had an actual phone conversation with my editor (hence having to find at least a semblance of pro writer brain) and I started writing again.

Not a lot, but writing.

The conversation was about rewrites vs. edits and when me and my writer brain would be available to provide these i.e. would I be able to do a bit of rewriting before MS was sent to Other Editor. I laughed maniacally, as you do. And I claimed I would have my brain back in October. (It's still August so October seemed impossibly far away during the phone call. Yes, I already have regrets.)

After this conversation, my honey suggested (more than once) that I start my "100 words a day" routine, the one I used to get back my writing brain after baby Eldest and the thesis drained me dry. I resisted this at first, much in the way that I often resist Panadol when I have a headache, despite knowing it would do me good. My main objection was that I had so *much* to write that a mere 100 words would be a drop in the ocean, so why put myself through that?

Yeah.

So I started on my daily 100 words, working my way through the less shiny half of Book #2. The first day back was ridiculously gruelling. I may have only stopped work a month ago, but what a month! Every word was now a struggle.

When I was done, I proudly tweeted that I had written 162 words. Many of those who replied/responded to me on Twitter or Facebook were vaguely congratulating (with a distinct tone of 'is she *serious*?'). Only a few really understood what it meant, and how much of an achievement it was to break through that barrier.

As I continued through the second half of this week,

writing 100ish words every day (never less than, no skipping a day) it really shocked me how hard it could be, carving out that moment of time and pushing myself into the novel. It was also frustrating, knowing that in my previous life, an average of 1000 words a day was normal.

There is no such thing as normal, with a newborn in the house.

Meagre though the 100 words a day is in fleshing out the novel, it is doing the trick. Most importantly, it is making sure that at least once a day, my novel (and not, for example, a certain Other Novel) is at the forefront of my mind. It's a good start.

WEEK FOUR

My 100 words a day continue. I've come up against a major problem, not so much with plot as with backstory I hadn't properly figured out, and decided I would allow my 100 words to be spent on what is essentially fanfic in my own universe (5 times Ashiol Xandelian broke and 1 time he didn't).

I was also called upon to write a synopsis/blurb for book 2 (aaargh, no way to do this without completely spoiling book 1 — trilogies suck!) and to come up with cover concepts for book 1. Hooray! I may not have a LOT of sleep under my belt, but for this week at least I am a Real Author™.

I bit the bullet and took my editor's kind hints about "flexibility" by requesting an extension on my deadline for Book #2. February 19th sounds so much better than January 1. I probably still won't be able to use November/NaNoWriMo to fastdraft the first 50 K of Book #3 before finishing up the polished Book #2 which I was really hoping for but... yes. Goalposts have moved.

I think I am officially a "working mum" now. Even if it's only for 20 minutes a day.

WEEK FIVE

More breakthroughs this week. I steadily continued working on my fanfic/backstory for the 100 words or more challenge, and started to feel the characters coming properly back to me. I had a couple of days in which I managed 200 or 300 words. Yeah, okay, that was kind of it for breakthroughs. But still.

I came up with cover concepts (a week late) and emailed them off to editor.

I also made practice cupcakes for Youngest's party and have been informed that this level of organisation is HUGE at five weeks post-birth. Personally I think it's a good thing I did the practice ones, otherwise I would have poisoned 30 of my nearest and dearest with an overdose of violet essence ...

WEEK SIX

Possibly because I have adapted more to this weird sleep system, (no more than 2-3 hours at a time, if I'm lucky) the writing came better this week. I had at least two 500 word days, in both cases when the writing was flowing. Real writing, too — I gave up on the fanfic backstory and submerged myself back in the novel, managing to fix scenes and actually do useful improvement instead of general messing about which, quite frankly, is what most of my "100 words a day" have consisted of.

I felt productive and sane and together. But ... by the end of the week I was back to putting plot points in brackets [insert devastatingly brilliant fight scene here]. Damn it. I also missed one day of writing due to extreme forgetfulness but I forgave myself, as it came after a 500 word day.

I met with my editor for coffee (two hours out of the house without baby, omg, talking about grown up things) and managed to hold sensible conversation. I think.

Did my taxes.

Had confirmation that a short story I co-wrote with my Swedish writing fairy has been accepted for a stories-for-children anthology.

Ooh, tried on the Safari (baby pouch) for the first time with Youngest and it still fits. Also it works. Can cuddle baby upright and keep hands free for typing. This will be useful later. ..

I am looking towards the end of September as the time I must Officially Have My Shit Together. The 30th is the date that my honey goes back to work. Why I have associated this date with said togetherness-of-shit I do not know. Surely being without that support I have taken for granted since Youngest's birth gives me permission to just collapse in a black hole of naps for a week.

And yet.

October is going to be the month of editing and rewriting book 1. The Publisher has been awesome about working around my life situation and making sure we all know what we are supposed to be doing, well in advance. It's comforting.

My novel (Book #2) word count currently stands at 94,500. I've managed 2000 words in 20 days — yes that is the bare minimum of 100 words a day, but the extras have been either on backstory or that short story. My brain is telling me I should be able to get to 100,000 by the end of the month. Obviously my brain is on drugs. It's not going to happen.

(My brain is also kind of hoping that NaNoWriMo[4] will still be possible in November. Brain is not to be trusted.)

WEEK SEVEN

Last week, I looked at the fact that I had 94,500 words down on my MS and blithely considered the possibility of reaching 100,000 by the end of the month. To be specific, by the 30th, which is the day my honey goes back to work and I am officially a stay-at-home-mum/writer on my *own*.

I then laughed at myself, because who was I kidding? I had a 6 week old baby, and in the first 20 days of the month I only managed 2000 words. And that was, frankly, a major achievement considering my brainspace and lack of sleep. To manage another 5,500 in the last 10 days a month felt impossible.

I continued on my 100 words a day method for a day or two, and then ... something clicked.

Why couldn't I go for it? I had to step up to a better work rate by October, and it was impractical to expect it to just miraculously happen on the day that my partner was no longer there to help with the kids.

So I sat down during a baby nap, cranked up the Big trilogy playlist, and wrote 1000 words in one sitting. My brain then melted out my ears for the rest of the day. But the point is — I did it. All this week I have written every day, with 500 words rather than 100 being my minimum. I've gone from 2000 words written this month to nearly 7000 — and at some point in the next two days, I will hit that 100K mark.

It's not a lot by my pre-baby standards, but it's looking pretty damn fine from here.

Pushing my boundaries this week was one of the best post-baby decisions I've made. I have been able to test my current ability levels, figuring out how and when I write best, and so on. My biggest challenge came yesterday, when a children's party and an afternoon nap meant that I still hadn't done my words by dinner time. In my old life that wouldn't have been a problem — churning out 1667 words after Eldest had gone to bed was more than possible.

But I don't live that life right now. By the time Eldest has gone to bed and we've managed to get Youngest at least pretending to sleep, I'm usually completely trashed. That's assuming that there is a gap between Eldest going to sleep (finally) and the baby waking up. Usually Youngest manages to miraculously choose the exact moment that her sibling loses consciousness to make a claim for freedom and mummy attention.

Last night, after big kid bedtime stories, I put the baby into my honey's hands, plugged in my earphones and played loud music at myself to churn out those 500 words. Five songs later, I had it done. Possible, yes, but way too hard on myself. I'll work harder to get the words done early in the day from now on. Baby-juggling is hard enough in the evening without work commitments as well.

I feel ridiculously proud of myself this week. Normality is in sight — or something approximating it. You can go a long way on 500 words a day.

(Oh yes, the latest edits for Crime Novel arrived, but that is a story for next week.)

WEEK EIGHT

Still a mother.
Still a writer.
This week, I:

- hit the 100K mark on the novel
- hated my novel
- had my first solo day at home with baby, after waving my honey off to work after his extended

cocktail of not-paternity-but-everything-else-leave
- had my second and third solo days as above
- changed a lot of nappies
- fell in love with my novel again
- spent a lot of time writing while joggling lovely baby rocker with foot (kicky music helps with this supermama skill)
- learned that when I go to the shops I do have to use baby pouch or stroller even if just nipping in for a few things. Baby is now *heavy*.
- did some other things, which I would remember now but can't, cos brain is all foggy
- zzzz
- finished major (hopefully last) copyedit for Crime Novel
- read and reviewed lotsa short stories
- read a lot of Gossip Girl books
- I would type more but my baby is trying to chew her way through my clothes.

WEEK NINE AND A HALF (obviously I wasn't going to stop at eight)

I've been writing away pretty well over the last week, managing my 500 word daily minimum. Which is good, because the stakes are high. My edits arrived from Big Publisher yesterday for Book #1 — and oh my, that is a big book, isn't it?

It's kind of lovely to be back to doing things the way they do in a traditional publishing house — editing directly on to a paper manuscript! Old school, and yet satisfying.

My friend Isabel and I had arranged to devote yesterday as pre-NaNo practice — and we weren't letting anything get in our way, even the fact that my entire family had called in sick. I callously left migraine-honey in charge of child-with-cold and ran away with the baby and my laptop.

We went to cafe-write first. Our favourite[5] was closed so we went to the juice bar and managed to write for an hour, fuelled by fruit smoothies (mmm pineapple mint).[6] Youngest managed about ten minutes in the pram before getting cranky, so I put her in the Safari baby pouch and joggled her to sleep while typing. Oh, that's what the wrist-rest is really for on my laptop — enables me to have a baby between me and it and still see the keyboard!

My total for the day was 1500 words plus — not quite a full NaNo daily word count but pretty damn swanky for a post-baby writing day. We even had time to open my exciting parcel and go 'ooooh' about the edit letters.

The excitement kept building. So much work to do, but the very best kind of work — the first real edit can be a brilliant process when you have an editor who really gets you, and wants to bring out the best in the book. Also, they want *maps*. I used to be one of those readers who was snobbish about books-what-have-maps-in but omg, maps! No one travels anywhere in my book, but the city is a hugely important feature of the story and the thought of someone translating my biro scribbles into a pretty-making Real Map … squeeee!

The glossary I put together to help me and any editors keep all the many worldbuilding details straight is going to be stripped of spoilers and added to the book! And I may get to put my calendar in there too — hooray!

I need to construct a massive to-do list. Apart from the edits themselves, there is the glossary edit to do, and I have to organise author photos, and get my notes/diagrams together for mapmaking and, and, and — why yes, this will be a full-time job over the next month or so. (Bounces madly)

My favourite part was looking at the projected timeline together — it's looking like it will be a June rather than July release — deciding the points at which we will have champagne to celebrate (there are a lot of those) and when we will have high tea... culminating of course in our grand bookshopcrawlfollowedbyhightea. The rules are you go from shop to shop, spotting as many copies of your book as possible, then collapse in a tearoom and embrace the smug. Then keep eating scones until the smug goes away and you can once more function as a normal person in society. Sometimes this takes a lot of scones...

While chatting, I realised that while I have been rattling away about Siren Novella to my internet peeps forever, I have not actually done much to let my real people know that I have a New Book Out Right Now. As Isabel put it: 'Tansy, you have not provided adequate foreshadowing for this!' I need to get on that.

I had the amazing realisation today that I only have three scenes to write and then the draft of #Book 2 is DONE. That puts me way ahead of schedule. Sure, the draft is about 20K short of where the final book needs to be, but that's what December is for. And January.

I can't tell you how hard it is not to just take the phone off the hook and write those scenes RIGHT NOW, but I have so many things that really have to be done today, that should have been done yesterday in fact, and, and, and —

Isabel promised me champagne on Thursday to celebrate my edit letter. If I finish the book before then as well, do I get cake?

Mmm, cake.

WEEK ELEVEN AND A HALF

My hefty book edits for Power and Majesty arrived last week. I went into a daze of 'they want maps!' (apparently the author has to provide these, who knew?)[7] 'they want to publish my glossary!' 'Whoa, author photos, better get on that,' 'I have DATES for everything between now and shipping to printers …' and promptly failed to start doing the actual edits for at least a week.

Well, I did finish off the draft of book 2 and then I had a cold. So I wasn't exactly slacking.

I was totally slacking.

This week, I have attacked the edits with gusto. I am overwhelmed by how good they are. It's lovely to have an editor who gets your book, is in sympathy with it, and manages to make completely rational and sensible suggestions to fix the problems you still knew were there. It's been an oddly soul-feeding experience.

The hard part is that I am still having to write new scenes — the only part of the book that is still not quite right is the earlier section, which covers many years (tricky) and I've always been treading the thin line between backstory/prologue and "get the hell on with the story." This section has always been the most divisive part of the book among my many readers, whose opinions have ranged from 'delete it and start later' to 'write more of it' and 'keep it just as it is.' Helpful, huh?

My editor has come down on the side of 'write more here, here and here,' and her suggestions have worked wonders. I've been writing new scenes for days, and I have three more to do before the first section is *done*. Then I just have to get on with the rest of the edits, and hope she wasn't kidding in her letter when she said it was pretty straightforward stuff from then on. I'm learning to trust her.

I hope she sticks around for the other two books. No one steal my editor, okay?[8]

The work is good, but hard. Book is making write better. I'm tired, strung out, and starting to stare at walls randomly. I haven't had enough sleep. I have no more childcare/school until Monday.

But the weather is getting warmer finally, and Show Day tomorrow means my honey home as well as an energetic 4-yr old, and the baby just keeps SMILING her little face off.

Really, I have little to complain about …

BACK IN THE PRESENT DAY

What did the 2020 Narrator learn from this immersion into productivity past? Wow, I think I was a more productive writer with a newborn baby on my lap than I am now. Harsh.

Keep on plugging away, even when it feels impossible. Some progress is better than no progress. Celebrate your wins. Tell your friends when you have a book released. Adjust your goals realistically. Accept help when it's offered. Don't compare yourself to other people, including the version of yourself who existed before you had kids. REQUEST DEADLINE AMENDMENTS WHERE POSSIBLE. Keep on writing.

The reward for writing is that you get to keep doing more of it.

The reward for parenting is … well, that's more complicated.

I'm sure I could come up with more terribly important advice about the balancing of writing and parenting and guilt and all those things, but… I have other things to write right now, and so do you.

Go get started.

1. Which actually became the Creature Court!
2. *Glares at novel with its sneaky, seductive ninja ways.*
3. 2020 Narrator: she didn't.
4. NaNoWriMo or National Novel Writing Month is a fun tradition where writers gather online and cheer each other on while writing 50,000 words during November. I've always done pretty well with it. It's the one time of year when my creative output matches my creative expectations. But … it only works for me during that month, and the consequences of "winning" my 50,000 words are that I basically nap through most of December.
5. Citrus Moon, the perfect hippie parent-friendly café, sadly now demolished. I mourn for it still.
6. Damn it, that juice bar is gone now too. I could really do with a smoothie.
7. There are times when it is incredibly helpful to have an endlessly patient mother who also has artistic skills. "Please draw maps of my complicated city which only really exists in my head" may be one of the toughest things I ever asked her to do but oh, the maps came out GREAT.
8. 2020 Narrator: no one stole her!

About the Author

Tansy Rayner Roberts is an award winning blogger, podcaster and fantasy author who lives in Tasmania with her family. She has a PhD in Classics and a particular attachment to Roman history, which infuses her work.

Tansy's books range from the light-hearted SFF like Tea and Sympathetic Magic and Musketeer Space to the darker and more epic Creature Court (the trilogy referenced in this book). She also writes cozy murder mysteries under the name Livia Day. Tansy is one of the co-hosts of the popular Verity! podcast, discussing Doctor Who with women around the world.

In 2013, Tansy won the Hugo for Best Fan Writer thanks

to the critical writing on her blog. This made her the first Australian woman ever to win a Hugo Award. She won it a second time in 2015 in the Best Fancast category with Galactic Suburbia.

Subscribe to her newsletter at tansyrr.com/tansywp/

- facebook.com/tansyrroberts
- twitter.com/tansyrr
- instagram.com/tansyrr
- goodreads.com/tansyrr
- patreon.com/tansyrr

Also by Tansy Rayner Roberts

THE CREATURE COURT TRILOGY

Power and Majesty

The Shattered City

Reign of Beasts

Cabaret of Monsters

Musketeer Space

Castle Charming

Tea and Sympathetic Magic

The Frost Fair Affair

Unreal Alchemy

Holiday Brew

Merry Happy Valkyrie

Love and Romanpunk

Girl Reporter

Pratchett's Women

AS LIVIA DAY

A Trifle Dead

Drowned Vanilla

Keep Calm and Kill the Chef

Thank You For Buying This Brain Jar Press Chapbook

To receive special offers, bonus content, and info on new releases and other great reads, visit us online at www.BrainJarPress.com

www.ingramcontent.com/pod-product-compliance
Lightning Source LLC
Chambersburg PA
CBHW020330010526
44107CB00054B/2063